The really, really, really useful
guide.

Number 4

How to
be a
Successful
Charity Shop

MIKE PEARCE

ISBN:10:1533187045
ISBN-13:978-1533187048

DEDICATION

This book is dedicated to all those who feel that they want to maximize sales and profit from donated items. Especially to those who like to look at new methods for promoting sales relevant to the area and community that they live in.

CONTENTS

Acknowledgments

MIKE PEARCE

ACKNOWLEDGEMENTS

The author would like to thank Christine Pearce for checking the manuscript. Also to all those who worked with me as volunteers for the great times working together and their ideas for increasing sales through display and realistic pricing.

INTRODUCTION

There are a huge variety of charity shops, many constrained by rules and regulations. This book contains many ideas to get the most out of charity shops based on the expertise and ideas of the volunteers who work in them. Many volunteers despair at the number of goods that do not reach the shop floor and have to be discarded and sold at a ridiculously low price to private contractors. This can be avoided by reducing prices, simple repairs or cleaning in some cases. It is important to display things well but huge expenditure on refits to retail standard also can change the clientele and cause a fall in profit. Hopefully the ideas presented in this book can form a basis for discussion at managerial level on ways forward for better satisfaction for staff and customers.

1 WHAT IS CHARITY?

Charity will always involve giving something, be it money goods or your time. Its origin comes from the Latin word Caritus meaning dear and in old English refers to love of ones fellow humans a form of philanthropy. The goods or money may originate from donations or raised by some other means e.g. sponsorship or collections. The aim is to help some living being or something that could be treasured and respected by a living thing. Charity edges on to Maslow's hierarchy of human needs, be it food, water, healthcare, clothing even a job and aims to help people up to self at the top of Maslow's pyramid. People with big families and those on benefits find them useful.

2 CHARITY SHOPS IN THE UK

There are estimated to be over 10,000 charity shops in the UK. The greatest of these are health related especially cancer and heart disorders. They provide jobs for over 15,000 volunteers

Animals also are supported by many charities, often several different ones for a particular animal such as cats and dogs. Wildlife also have numerous charities especially those to help a particular species which is suffering in its environment or is endangered.

Nobody knows what someone will buy. Sight of an object triggers an urge to purchase something useful or just even for ornamentation. It might even be a present for someone else (often new or unused items may be in the shop). So have a good look round and rummage into different sections.

Charity shops are hugely beneficial. They help to attract people to other businesses despite what some people may say. They give people new skills such as retail and teamwork as well as the chance to meet new people. They can help prevent loneliness bringing people out from their homes, especially the elderly who also can feel they are contributing to society.

3 KINDS OF CHARITY SHOPS

There are many different specialisations and broad-spectrum shops. Specialist shops can include more upmarket goods such as retro or top of the range furniture. Some specialist shops can be clothes, or books or furniture. Others don't take some items but specialise in others. While many take all donations in whatever state they are in and sort or display as much as possible. Some shops have bought in new goods, others lease with dealers or the public who produce items such as crafts and offer a share of the profits. Charity shops, by recycling, contribute to reducing carbon dioxide emissions.

4 ACCESS-RACKS AND SHELVING

- Access is extremely important. Too often racks of clothes are placed in the centre of the shop leaving little space to walk through, especially if someone is standing in the aisle
- Avoid inaccessibility to the windows with things on the floor in front of them
- Try and avoid high shelves with pictures on especially
- Make sure book displays are at eye level and above. No one likes creeping down on the floor to see what books are there
- Display cases are good especially for valuable items and jewellery

5 ANIMAL CHARITY SHOPS

- Some shops allow dogs, in others are more restrictive. Bowls of water may be placed in front of the shop or near the door in hot weather
- Some animal charity shops offer biscuits to any dog coming inside. This definitely helps to form good relationships between staff and customer and help business
- Some shops offer advice to people on looking after health or protecting animals in leaflet form or by indicating places to contact
- Some dogs will settle down when their owners go round the shop. Some shop may have a bar attached to a wall to tie dogs to
- Rescue charities may have pictures of missing animals and also give consolation or advice. They also can put your animal onto a lost and found web site. These shops also can be linked to helping to find homes for all kinds of animals and pets
- These shops may also have items related to housing or controlling animals, collars leads and beds as well as a good stock of old blankets for dog

6 ART, CRAFT AND PICTURES

- Good craft and art can attract good prices
- One can also sell handmade sculpture if it looks professional
- Bronzes and metal work can form good centre pieces in the shop window often attracting passers by
- There are many massed produced pictures often of flowers which may even turn up in bulk at charity shops as have not been sold in shops. These need to be sold at low prices or just for the frame
- Where pictures are damaged or faded from too much exposure then they can be removed and the frames sold separately
- Pictures need to be displayed on walls with good attachments or on top of shelves or leant against objects on the floor. They can also be placed in a box but not too tightly packed to prevent breakages
- Small pictures can be fitted behind bric a brac in the window or on the shelves
- Large mirrors are better displayed on the floor and this is safer as they are often heavy
- Original water colours or oil paintings will always command a better price than prints.

- Local scenes can attract a decent price
- Some local artists can link up work with charity shops to share the profits
- Artists or crafts people can also be encouraged to work on their products in the shop, even if only for a short time

7 BAGS AND PURSES

- Bags look good hanging on wall pegs and can be hung behind the till on the wall
- Bags can also be placed on tables
- Important to check zips and clasps on bags and purses as on clothing to make sure they work and also the cleanliness inside
- Dirty bags, as with purses, can be washed even steamed if necessary. Leather can be polished and scuff marks brought back up with polish
- Often there are many evening bags donated of many styles. It is important not to put too many out at once
- For knapsacks and cases/suitcases it is important gain to check zips and make sure wheels are functional

8 BIG ITEMS

- Big items are best placed at the back or front of the shop near the window. Sports equipment, rolls of carpet, cabinets and CD racks can take up a lot of space. Prices need to be realistic to make sure they are sold as soon as possible. Stained-glass panels are very popular
- Need to avoid taking in too large items in a small shop as you may be stuck with them for a long time
- Often branches of charity shops may have other shops which specialise and have the space for bigger items

9 BOOKS, CARDS AND JIGSAWS

- With the decline in reading books, but an increased flood of popular novels some charity shops are overstocked. Some even have warehouses full

- It is important when displaying books to have them in subject order if not novels i.e. cookery, science fiction etc. Novels can be put into author order if someone is dedicated to do this but often some authors exceed the space than others making book arrangement difficult

- Often there are many oversize books. Even if these are thicker and with more attractive covers one must ensure that prices are not unrealistic in order to sell them

- Where a series exists e.g. Mills and Boon they can be sold as sets. Some books if non sellers can be tied together and even used to put in the garden as homes for creepy crawlies. Some companies are doing this on a large scale with piles of books tied and secured together like walls for bees etc. to make their homes. They say this encourages predators so plants are protected from pests

- Many books are written inside, with bent corners, browning at the sides or marked in some way. These are often discarded and sold in bulk for a ridiculously cheap price. Some books in this state are still valuable so care needs to be taken

- Some organisations have a price list for all books and will not reduce their prices but in the current climate they need to get smarter and do as others and sell them at a very low price or a certain number for a low price. The market is still out there but not at unrealistic prices

- Old maps and visitor guides are not redundant and can be sold if the price is right.

- Use the display window for interesting or rare books and put relevant books out linked to national or local events

- Some shops have cards on display near the entrance or till

- Some charities have specific charity cards produced for Christmas or even birthdays

- It is good to enlist some card makers or link up to a local course making cards so as to have these in the shop and share the profits

- If selling playing cards, need to check content as with all games to check they are fully complete. To find a card missing can be a real bug bear for customers

- Postcards can be displayed in a box or in plastic sleeves
- Jigsaws are often popular for some people. If in a plastic bag all pieces could be there. Often volunteers may like to make jigsaws and take them home to check the number of pieces
- Jigsaws can be displayed on higher shelves as, if they did fall, they would cause little damage
- Often older jigsaws such as the Victory series, even if the box is slightly damaged can be valuable.
- It is good to have a jigsaw event and bring out a wide variety of choice at an affordable value.
- Jigsaws can be placed in a cage basket near the entrance to help with sales
- It may be useful to keep in contact with senior citizens' clubs who may use jigsaws or jigsaw clubs

10 CANDLES, NIGHT LIGHTS AND AROMATIC OILS

- Candles are always popular especially if in good condition and long
- Candles can be used in the presentation of candle holders
- Make sure you do not display candles in the window as they will bend over under the heat of the sun
- Night lights are not expensive and can be placed in holders when donated to help sell them
- Night lights are also used in aromatic china burns to evaporate essential oils. If a night light is included one can raise the price slightly

- Non bees wax candles can be of poor quality so need pricing accordingly

11 CHILDREN'S TOYS

- To check on the value of old teddies one can link to the bear society
- Knitted items can be a problem as they don't have a CE number on them. Formally these could not be sold but they can be sold as dog toys making sure that any glass plastic or metal attachments are removed such as eyes
- There are often many small items included with donations of toys. These can be put in a basket and sold separately for the same price
- Ensure a wide selection of different toys are on display at prices that are affordable. Very few boot fair stall do not have one toy or another sold at very low prices. People will expect lower prices on toys which today are seen as a disposable commodity
- Many preschool toys are common in the shops and are popular with mothers.
- Check toys are not fakes and they have a CE mark on them
- Give toys a good clean where they have become mucky
- Avoid toys or items which have been in children's mouths such as teethers or dummies unless they are packaged as new
- Check all pieces of games are present or parts of some toys which are often missing

12 CHINA

- Plates left over from tea and dinner services can build up in charity shops. Half a dozen good large plates are saleable
- Tea sets are not always complete but try and match cups and saucers as a set of two or three
- Run the end of your finger carefully around the rims of china to make sure there are no chips
- Large colourful pots and vases tend to sell well
- China figures of people or animals give better value if well painted and realistic
- Put larger objects at the a back of display and smaller ones in front
- Some shops are recognised by putting tea sets at reasonable prices in the window. One needs to continue a trend so that people can see what's on offer
- Always make sure some mugs are on display

13 CLOTHES

It's not worth spending loads of money in a standard store for a one off occasion so look in a charity shop first.

Men's

- Men's clothes are often of good quality, many items as new as they are hardly worn
- Ties and bow ties have lost their popularity but this depends where you live. Display is important for these and these can be put onto mannequins to display
- It is essential to have sales now and then to move clothing. Correct sizes are important and a room should be supplied to try these on if needed
- If a female clothed manikin is in the shop it's a good idea to have a manikin clothed in men's clothing as well
- Always check the pockets of men's coats to avoid some embarrassing items which have been known to have been found
- Steaming will improve the appearance of suits and thick coats immensely

<u>Women's</u>

- These form the largest amount of donations and need to be related to seasonal times. It is no use putting out heavy coats or thick jumpers in the height of summer
- Some charity shops arrange their clothes according to colour in the hope that people are looking to where their favourite colour is displayed
- Older clothes can be displayed in specific retro shops where higher prices can be charged.
- Elaborate wedding dresses can be displayed at good prices which are still way below those charged if purchased new
- Women's clothes can attract people into the shop when placed in the window on dummies. It is important to put quality or attractive coloured clothes in this spot
- Steaming garments, especially trousers and coats, will always improve appearance

14 COSMETICS AND PERFUMES

- Often donations include make up bags with many items included. These need to be checked for date and examined for contents to see they have not separated out or only partially full
- Perfumes and aftershave are often a good seller. Sometimes expensive perfumes are donated and even if not full they can be sold. Even empty perfume bottles are saleable
- Cosmetics for use on the face should be discarded, especially if previously used.
- Compacts, if used, can be sold especially if old
- Beware of cosmetic sets with liquids or powders in which may be toxic or cause allergies

15 DISPLAY OR NOT TO DISPLAY

The window

- The window is what you are. Put in uninteresting bland items then this is what they think you sell
- Include a raised shelf along the window if you can, to maximise your display area
- Make the centre of window your best display. Cut glass often is very attractive in bright sunlight
- Put expensive items in the window to maximise viewing
- Keep to national and local and seasonal events in the window for people to relate to. If it's a religious event, no matter what sect, exploit this to the full
- It is good to have mannequins in the window, not only to display clothes, but to include jewellery and scarves as well as a hat on top even if there is no head
- Mannequins can be placed one either side of the window display. Some windows can have several mannequins in a row say five. You can alternate the sexes so as to provide a selection of clothes, scarves etc.

- Mannequins should be placed behind the main display in the window if there is room but make sure there is access to the window

- Small tables can be included either side in the window or centrally so as to include more items in the window. Some shops put small clothes or doylies on these to make them more attractive

- When items are sold in the window transfer valuable and attractive items from inside the shop to the window

- In the window you can actually create scenes using mannequins. A family group seated around a table with attractive items for sale scattered around the table and at the side, can make these items more attractive to buy

In the shop

- Some shops colour code items. Even if you do not colour code clothes try and keep similar coloured glass and china together for effect

- Try and display related things together and keep to these areas so the public always knows where to look

- Don't give minority plain items priority display space. Choose the attractive and

unusual as well as the decorative and
expensive

- People like to rummage through things for a
bargain. One can have a basket with items all
at one low price. Goods can also be placed in
a basket at a reduced price e.g. scarves, books,
CDs
- If things on display don't sell then reduce the
price to clear them, don't recycle them for a
lower value

16 E-BAY

- Antiques and speciality items can make a
better profit on eBay
- Collections which should not be split up also
are better suited for e-Bay
- Gold silver and some antique brasses and
semi-precious stones can sell well on e-Bay
- Some things are numerous on e-Bay and may
be better sold within the shop
- Coins stamps, collections of porcelain, old
cameras, signed items and memorabilia can be
better served by e-Bay
- Volunteers should put possible items aside for
the appointed e-bay person to see. The
manager can also decide which items sell best
on e-Bay from past experience

17 ELECTRICAL AND FURNITURE

- It is important that any electric equipment leaving the shop is PAT tested or checked through other approved testing procedures. Faulty equipment can be dangerous for customers and items may have been given away because they are faulty
- It is so important to test battery driven equipment, even toys, as they may often have been donated as broken
- Check inside the battery box, batteries may have leaked and rusted or dissolved away the terminals and the item will no longer work with batteries
- Even some of the well-known charity shops in the UK still sell faulty electrical toys which are very attractive in structure and price
- There needs to be an assigned section for goods. Large items such as freezers and fridges need to be checked against current restrictions
- Watches often come without batteries. Batteries can be purchased at cheap stores for replacement
- Old, out-dated electrical equipment can be sold as retro etc. for display but plugs must be removed

- It is not always easy to test electrical equipment so a returns policy needs to be in place
- Taking in furniture into the shop can reduce the floor space available. There need to have specific rules in place for certain items that can be accepted. Also with large furniture there is the problem of delivery
- However, some shops specialise in furniture and large electrical goods
- Small furniture can sell well and make good profit
- With a clean and a polish (some furniture may still have a layer of yellow nicotine on its surface as with pictures) this can add extra value
- Broken furniture can be repaired in some cases so a tool kit and various glues need to be held in the shop
- All furniture as with any wooden item, needs to be examined for wood worm. If there is no dust in the holes and they are dark internally this can mean they have been treated. It is safer to state on the label that there is a possibility of worm in some cases as these items may spread the insects into a person's home

18 FOOD

- Some charity shops are able to sell food items from an overspill from an allotment as well as flowers
- It is most important to check the quality of food items given especially sell by dates. This is important such as when a gift set with chocolates and a wine glass are in packaging and would make a good display but the chocolates sell by date could be a few years ago
- It is great to have somewhere to make tea and with a sink. It is also useful to have a fridge even if it is a very small portable on
- A manager who makes tea on the arrival of new volunteers sets a good friendly impression
- A good supply of tea coffee and milk should be available for volunteers. Some shops restrict taking coffee into the main shops but some may like to drink theirs there especially as to keep the person on the till company.
- It could be good to have cakes on special occasions as well as arrange small outings for meals for volunteers now and again

19 FREEBIES

- Do freebies have any effect of value added?
- Free pens and carrier bags for bought goods can satisfy people as well as promote the charity
- A bowl of mints or sweets is also good if volunteers don't eat them all
- In some charity shops some goods which are not saleable can be put in racks outside and offered free. Examples could be plastic garden pots and soft toys which may be in abundance. Previous goods which were freebies can also be dispensed with in this way
- Books not top of the range can also be given free at certain times to free up space in the shop for other more profitable item
- Leaflets and magazines about the charity are very important especially where they give examples of where the money is used.

20 GARDEN EQUIPMENT

- China plant pots and pot holders are often common. These can be washed out before sale and even if stained can be sold at a lower price
- Chemicals for the garden, as for medical treatments are best discarded for safety reasons. Some of these may now be banned from use
- Garden equipment needs to be displayed together in a standard place in the shop
- Need to ensure cutting tools are still functional

22 GIFT AID

- It is important not to force this on people
- If you don't pay tax the tax man will give it to charity and take the money from you
- Ensure labels are printed out with the goods as soon as possible and placed with the goods

21 GLASS

- Every shape and size of glass can be donated coloured or not
- Better shaped or engraved glasses warrant a higher price than plain glasses
- Some shops will discard a single glass and only sell pairs, which is a shame as single glasses can be reduced right down
- Sets of colourful glasses or bowls vases can be put in the window. This is even more attractive if half are the same colour.
- It is important to distinguish plain cut glass from crystal
- Often decanters may come with the wrong stopper. This can be tested by turning the decanter upside down with the top in. If it is not original it will not make a perfect fit and drop out

23 HATS

- One can get a wonderful variety of hats. These can be chosen to relate to events and seasons
- They can be displayed on the top of manikins even if they do not have heads
- Fascinators are always elaborate and even volunteers have good fun trying them on and can buy them
- Colourful hats can be displayed in the window to attract passers-by. Often hats can be bought for weddings

24 INPUT

- Input will normally always exceed output
- January is big for donations from clear outs and unwanted gifts as is the day after boot fairs
- Items come in from a move, a bereavement, after a boot fair, or just a clear-out
- You can buy in goods or stock from shop closures but some customers see this as moving away from the true charity shop and competing with other shops with brand new items
- Beware, often charity shops are seen as a way of getting rid of rubbish. This is especially

true where a house clearance is required because of an imminent move. The charity shop could be charged for taking rubbish to the tip

- Although difficult, it is important to move goods on. If they are not going to sell they are not going to sell

- Dirty, stained clothes, broken items and items not working, in a perfect world could be cleaned or repaired but the pace and amount of donations can often prohibit such practice. Each charity shop should set up a minor repair unit and all the regular items for cleaning and polishing so as to get items out where possible

- Beware of goods left outside the shop door when it is close. These can be stolen or even money can be put through the door where items have been taken

- If goods are gift aid items ensure labels are attached and items are recorded on the system

- Often china may have a small crack or nick on them. Reflect this in the price. Older items can still have good value in this condition

- Check older items and marked items for a sense of value from the internet but realise you may not get the same price in your shop. You have to be realistic

25 JEWELLERY

- Jewellery can be displayed in many ways. Necklaces can hang over the side of boxes or from special jewellery hooks
- A black or even red background can show off jewellery to best advantage. A piece of velvet material cut from a piece of unwanted clothing can be ideal
- Small baskets can be used for small jewellery
- Glass cases can be used for valuable jewellery and placed in the window.
- A frame of wire netting can also be hung up on the wall and jewellery displayed on this
- Mannequins can also have jewellery pinned all over them to give a wise choice
- Important if you say silver on a label that it is really silver not another metal
- Children's jewellery can be placed in a children's section
- Lighting can enhance jewellery as well as mirrors underneath. These can add sparkle if stones or silver is present

26 KITCHENALIA

- Kitchen items have proved very popular
  Pots and pans are always good sellers and are
  often still in good condition when donated
- Cutlery can be sold in sets. Many sets of fish
  knives and forks in their boxes often appear
  but their usefulness these days is limited
- Odd cutlery can be displayed loose in a
  basket. Knives, spoons and forks can be
  displayed in a small pot or basket so that
  individual ones can be chosen by customers
- Sharp kitchen knives or choppers need to be
  in a safe protected place or cabinet to prevent
  accidents
- Badly scratched metal trays can be sold at very
  low prices as trays for plants
- Silver plated or silver items are better cleaned,
  even if partially, before being displayed with
  brass
- Elaborate stainless steel items can be donated
  by small restaurants

27 MUSIC

- To play music you may have to have a licence which can be expensive
- Some staff/customers like music but this depends on the kind of music
- Many staff like the radio playing for company which helps time pass when on one's own especially in winter when custom is reduced
- Some music can be chosen to match the kind of shop e.g. retro or calm music for boutiques
- Sheet music especially old music can be very collectible. Even if the inner pages are in poor condition, damaged front covers can be framed to make an attractive display

28 NON SALE ITEMS

- Some things won't sell and there is a need every week to change stock
- If unsaleable items were not collected by a contractor for some profit you would have to pay someone to take them away
- Beware of private contractors who collect clothing so they don't reach charity shops
- A lot of non-sale goods go overseas but are not distributed freely as people still have to pay for them. Even some of these goods turn up in local markets in this country from recycling merchants
- Labels can reflect the week in the year to say how long things have been on display
- Items can be shunted between shops
- Some charity shops do not take certain items and would love to donate them to other charity shops
- One can contact organisations to take away surplus donations. Returns on this is low, so try and reduce prices before dumping stock
- There is a gap in the market for collecting items discarded and repairing or cleaning them for resell or export
- Vintage should never go to waste, especially clothes. Also remember that some goods can

come into fashion again and also depend on the season or occasions

- It is always important to have a sale rail

29 OUTPUT

- Till receipts give an idea of sales but are often difficult to analyse. Not all income is profit. You need to compare with other charity shops Profit can be skewed by selling a large piece of furniture for example. Over fifty pence in every pound can go on the expense of running a shop
- It is difficult sometimes to know what sells well as depends on kind of people, time of year, weather and numerous factors
- Volunteers can have an idea of what goes well so ask them
- You can gear the kinds of goods to the people who commonly come in as well as to events
- It is important to get goods out into the shop and change regularly if not sold Reintroduce them again at a lower price or at the right time such as school holidays
- Some people who have worked in retail say the shop is too cluttered if too many goods are out. This is unrealistic as if they are

displayed well the game is to maximise profit and people are not going to buy things hidden in a room at the back waiting for a space to be vacant to put them in

- Get large items e.g. furniture, out as soon as possible. Furniture can be a big seller and achieve higher prices than other goods
- Aim to make a sale of any goods rather than dispose of it in recycling. Reduce price very low if not bought after a week
- Can increase output by the quality of goods on display and good customer service.
- Get volunteers to talk to their customers and compliment them on what they are buying or explain more about the item
- You can even say to the person on the till what they are putting out. People listen and are interested
- Make sure people get a bargain. There are a lot of cheap outlet shops now out there for all things at low prices. You can even reduce it slightly to increase customer satisfaction and customer return. Often by reducing they may also look at other items in the shop and buy them as well
- Make sure that people don't link your shop with high prices at full retail prices for other's cast offs

- Be prepared to check stock for a request. This is added value
- Can put new or nearly new on an item to attract confidence in a buy
- By reducing and crossing out the original price with a red line this can stimulate a purchase
- Don't overprice all your items or this reputation will ensure customers do not return. It's also harder to recoup a profit with things at a higher price but you can always reduce them
- Make sure the branding is good and the visual image of quality is exhibited
- Note charities can be involved with fraud by some staff or external individuals who may raise funds falsely from the charity's name
- Notices in the window of sales and events are beneficial. One can also put a notice board outside
- Beware of change. Check demographic groups and make sure you don't abandon your usual clientele

30 PROBLEMS

- There is no insurmountable problem in a charity shop. Assistant managers or key people can always find a way round, as can other volunteers
- Common problems are still not working, ringing up wrong amount, return, complaints about pricing
- Important every day when displaying or working to look at health and safety and risk assessment e.g. things placed up high
- Don't give up volunteering if something has gone wrong. It's a learning curve and you can bet your bottom dollar it won't be the only time that someone makes a mistake

31 SHARING WITH DEALERS OR THE PUBLIC ON GOODS

- Some shops liaise with dealers bringing them in to value or even allow them to buy items before the public see them. This can often reduce the quality of goods in the shop, the shop being left with worthless items and cast offs from the dealer

- It is often useful to link with dealers, especially where some items are particularly difficult to sell such as books

- Dealers also can help with valuation and authenticity e.g. deciding on whether a thing is ivory or not

- Some shops do a fair share where a percentage of the profits goes to someone or a dealer who has brought something in. Often higher priced items are only accepted. The share may be 50% but some dealers would prefer slightly more

- Difficulties with fair share occur where items which have been handmade such as jewellery, are brought in. The materials used in their construction may not be covered by the price on the label and to put the price up higher would mean they are much more expensive than elsewhere

- With fair share a contract should be set up with the owner and you must be able to contact them if a lower offer is made. Make sure any small amounts of damage are recorded o the contract to prevent the owner claiming for damages later
- If goods are not sold after a few months they should be asked to reduce their price, possibly donate them or come and take them away
- One also has to be careful when accepting made goods not to flood the shop with them so as to exclude other saleable items. If many are similar then examples can be on display or an album showing the variety of goods available

32 RECORDS, TAPES AND CD'S

- Vinyl is making a comeback
- Where LPs were previously sold at very low prices and even made into flower pots they now can command a decent price
- Some shops have experts who can value LPs, some records demanding up to £30 and above
- Old pre-war and wartime LPs can also be valuable if by specific artists and are not mainly classical types
- Small recording tapes in their plastic boxes are currently not sold by many charity shops as many no longer have players for them. This also goes for cassette tapes. Some people still have players for these as well as CDs. Places such as hospitals and care homes are typical users. Both kinds of cassettes can be purchased cheaply and not all cassettes have made it onto the CD.
- CDs as with DVDs now flood charity shops. One must look out for pirate copies so as not to sell them. These can be identified from the sleeves and the kind of discs used. CD/video

given free in papers etc. can be sold as a donation.

- Some CDs/DVDs are perfectly playable but scratched on the underside. These can be sold at a lower price in a separate section
- One needs to be realistic on prices for DVDs and CDs as low cost shops sell similar items

33 SHOES

- These can be displayed or racks. or under hanging clothes at the side of the shop
- It is good to have a chair in the shop for people to sit down and try on shoes as well as partners having a rest while one of them looks around
- Cleaning shoes can add to their attractiveness so stocks of polish, cloths and brushes need to be kept in the shop
- Shoes can be placed on display next to jewellery can criss- cross shoes for greater effect

34 STORAGE

- Storage places can become a place to hide away things which never reach the shop floor year after year
- If you have a cellar or many storage rooms upstairs make a point of taking things out every day to reduce the contents
- Keep things together in storage and save things for special seasonal celebrations or local events e.g. folk week or Dickens's festivals, Christmas, Halloween etc.
- Make sure that paper items and books are not stored near windows or in damp areas.
- Make use of racks in storage room to maximise storage space
- Some items too big to display can be stored. However if they cannot be displayed in the shop without difficulty, a notice can be placed on the window to prevent receiving such things as prams, pushchairs and large gym equipment

35 VOLUNTEERS AND THE UNUSUAL

- Some objects originate from overseas and can be very attractive. An example of this is a shell lampshade made up of several hundreds of shells
- Often wood carvings are donated and are difficult to price but similar items can be found on the internet
- Volunteers can be stumped by some unusual objects but someone somewhere may know what the object is used for
- You need to be careful where some objects look broken or rubbish as they may be valuable art pieces and command a good price
- Plastic flowers may look ready for the bin but a wash in the sink with washing up liquid can transform them to their former beauty
- Some people may have donated items from nature e.g. exotic shells, corals, seed pods, fossils which you may think are valueless. This may not be the case as someone always can be interested in anything

- People may have a passion for different things and by taking their phone number you can tell them if things are in the shop. Often people need knitting needles, some collect sewing machines, others buy timetables or pop music magazines from the past
- You will often get collections of different china, plaster or plastic items. Large collections- even hundreds of pigs, frogs, cats, dogs, bells, spoons, thimbles or elephants can arrive in your shop
- Charities may be resistant to change but if set out as a proposal and showing the benefits these ideas can be taken up There are businesses available to visit other charities and learn about their organisations

36 WOODEN OBJECTS

- Wooden objects may not be some people's cup of tea. Wooden bowls of all shapes and sizes can be donated
- Carving can sometimes crop up, often originating from South East Asia or Africa. Often these are made from light woods and may not be that attractive for customers. Many of the mask like carvings are tourist wares but even old pieces of these can be valuable
- It is important to try to ascertain the age of a wooden object. As with some metal objects there may be a build-up of cleaning material in some of the joins or depressions
- Hardwoods with good weight can suggest some age especially if darkened
- Poor carving may indicate machine carving but rough carving can be old
- There are many items made from bamboo or coconuts. Again prices on these must be realistic as demand for these can be low
- Many walking sticks are run of the mill and need to be priced reasonably for purchase by

the elderly. Others may have carved handles
or silver bands and good prices can be
achieved for these.

Other booklets in the really, really, really useful series include:

1. How to be a Successful Business Weed
2. How to Deal with Life's Snakes and Ladders
3. Pens for Pops

Other books by Mike Pearce:

1. Pattern for Purpose- God's and Man's designs
2. Red Fred Cell and Friends
3. Human Termites eat London
4. Pigeons Splat London
5. Glass Anemones Tentacle-ize London
6. Tuppeny Hangover
7. I am Termite
8. The littlest Oyster
9. Bits and Bobs
10. The Shell Man
11. Cats at Christmas
12. Tails, Tales
13. Trust-Nothing but a Must
14. In a Dark, Dark Corner was the Holy Ghost
15. The shell lady
16. Captain Grottbuster versus the Grey World
17. London's Nemesis(Trilogy of 3,4 and 5 above
18. Saved by Angels (Trilogy of 6,8 and 14 above)
19. The World of Wax

ABOUT THE AUTHOR

Dr Mike Pearce is a scientist interested in behaviour. He also was a lecturer in human biology and health at a college in Canterbury, Kent.

www.ingramcontent.com/pod-product-compliance
Lightning Source LLC
Chambersburg PA
CBHW070406190526
45169CB00003B/1135